PERSEVERANCE PERSONIFIED

THE RISE OF ANUMULA REVANTH REDDY

KONDA MURALI

This book is dedicated to
Sri Anumula Revanth Reddy,
Honourable Chief Minister of Telangana,
whose dedication, vision, and unwavering efforts
inspired this work.

With the inspiration drawn from his leadership,
which has illuminated the future of Telangana,
this humble piece of writing is sincerely dedicated.

Konda Murali, Author
Cell: 9441431090

Contents

Contents

Foreword

Purpose of the book

The purpose of the book is to explore the skills and factors that enabled Anumula Revanth Reddy to rise to the position of Chief Minister of Telangana in a remarkably short period. It highlights how the people of Telangana recognized him as the most suitable choice for the role of Chief Minister.

The book also provides an in-depth analysis of the remarkable political journey of Anumula Revanth Reddy, exploring the leadership qualities, strategic decisions, and interpersonal skills that have shaped his rise in politics. By examining key aspects such as visionary thinking, crisis management, communication abilities, and emotional intelligence, this book aims to highlight the multifaceted qualities that have enabled Revanth Reddy to effectively navigate the complex political landscape.

Through a detailed exploration of his leadership style, the book offers insights into how adaptability, innovation, and strategic planning play a crucial role in shaping political success. Furthermore, the book delves into the importance of public perception and image building, as well as the role of influence and networking in securing a political position. With case studies and milestones marking pivotal moments in his career, this book serves as a comprehensive guide to understanding the key factors that contributed to Anumula Revanth Reddy's rise to power and his ongoing impact on the political landscape.

Preface

Background of the Chief Minister

Anumula Revanth Reddy, a prominent politician was born on November 8 in 1969 in Kondareddipally village, located in Vangoor mandal of Nagarkurnool district. This village falls under the Achampet constituency and was situated in the erstwhile Mahaboobnagar district. Revanth Reddy was born to Narasimha Reddy and Ramachandramma, who were both farmers. He was the fourth child in a family of eight siblings, including one daughter and seven brothers.

Revanth Reddy's family epitomizes the timeless values of togetherness and support, thriving in the midst of modern challenges. United under one roof in a joint family setup, they share not only the joys but also the struggles of life, bound together by a deep sense of affection. Despite belonging to the middle class, their unity and hard work have propelled each brother to a position of success.

In an age where technological advancements often drive families apart, the Reddys stand as a beacon of familial unity, defying the norm by remaining tightly knit. During Revanth Reddy's electoral journey, his brothers-Thirupathi Reddy, Kondal Reddy, Jagadeeshwar Reddy and Krishna Reddy- stood firmly by his side, extending unwavering support and actively campaigning on his behalf, showcasing the enduring strength of their bond and collective spirit.

Revanth Reddy's achievement of taking the oath as Chief Minister filled his sister's heart with immense pride. She expressed her belief that his dedication and hard work had finally borne fruit, and she was confident that he would fulfil his responsibilities with utmost sincerity. She spoke fondly of the people of Telangana, considering them fortunate to have Revanth Reddy as their leader. She assured that they were in safe hands under his capable leadership. Her words reflected not only familial pride but also a deep sense of trust and admiration for her brother's abilities and commitment to serving the people.

Since childhood, Revanth Reddy possessed a natural affinity for befriending the elders and engaging with youth associations, showcasing his sociable nature and inclusive mindset devoid of any caste or creed distinctions. His circle of close friends extended across various communities, reflecting his ability to connect with people from diverse backgrounds.

His mother nurtured lofty dreams for her sons envisioning him as a leader destined for greater heights, perhaps even as a ruler in Delhi. Her blessings have indeed manifested in his journey, culminating in his ascension to the role of Chief Minister.

The adage, "Child is father of the man" finds resonance in the life of Revanth Reddy, where his upbringing continues to shape his character and actions as an adult. The foundation laid during his formative years profoundly influences his present persona. Blessed with a secure and nurturing childhood, the impact of his parents' upbringing on his life journey is unmistakable. Today Revanth Reddy stands as evidence to enduring effects of a stable and loving environment, emerging as a morally and emotionally resilient individual. The security and the support he received during his formative years have fortified him, enabling him to navigate life's challenges with confidence and integrity. His upbringing serves as a guiding light, shaping his values and decisions as he assumes roles of leadership and responsibility in society.

Revanth Reddy's educational journey began in his native village of Kondareddipally, where he received his elementary education, laying the groundwork for his academic pursuits. Continuing his quest for knowledge, he moved to Thandra village for high school studies, demonstrating a commitment to learning even at a young age.

His passion for science and drawing led him to choose the Bi.P.C group during his intermediate education, a decision driven by his keen interest in these subjects. Enrolling in a private college in Wanaparthy town for his intermediate studies, Revanth Reddy quickly distinguished himself as a leader among his peers. Serving as a class representative (C.R), he exhibited exemplary leadership skills, effectively managing classroom affairs with tact and diligence.

His proactive approach to organizing events and celebrations further showcased his leadership qualities, with his artistic talent evident in the captivating drawings adorning boards and banners, leaving a lasting impression on guests and fellow students alike. Revanth Reddy's early academic years were marked by a blend of academic excellence, leadership prowess, and artistic flair, laying the groundwork for his future endeavours.

After relocating to Hyderabad for his higher education, Revanth Reddy enrolled at A.V College, affiliated with Osmania University, marking a significant chapter in his academic journey. It was here that his innate qualities began to shine through particularly upon joining the ABVP organization, where his leadership skills blossomed.

As a prominent student leader, he tirelessly worked to address numerous issues affecting the student community, often leading protests and advocating for change. Despite his busy schedule, Revanth Reddy found solace and creative expression in his passion for drawing, dedicating his evenings to this pursuit. His artistic talent did not go unnoticed, earning him numerous accolades and praise for his contributions to the college community.

Upon completing his degree, he ventured into entrepreneurship, establishing a printing press that operated successfully for a period of time. Subsequently, he transitioned into business ventures, achieving financial success and stability. Harnessing his prosperity for the greater good, Revanth Reddy embarked on philanthropic endeavours, utilizing his resources to make a positive impact on society. His journey from student activism to entrepreneurship and philanthropy reflects a trajectory marked by determination, leadership, and a commitment to serving others.

Revanth Reddy's affection for Geetha Reddy, the niece of the renowned Congress politician Jaipal Reddy, initially faced resistance from Geetha's family. Despite efforts to keep them apart, Revanth remained steadfast in his desire to marry Geetha. In the harmonious year of 1992, Revanth and Geetha embarked on a journey of love, exchanging vows and cementing their bond in marriage. Their union was blessed by their families, marking the beginning of a lifelong companionship built on love, trust, and mutual respect.

In 1993, Revanth and Geetha's joy multiplied when their precious daughter, Nymisha Reddy, was born. She quickly became the center of their world, bringing immense happiness and love into their lives. Nymisha was adored as daddy's little princess, captivating their hearts with her infectious laughter and sweet presence.

As a family, Revanth and Geetha navigated life's journey hand in hand, guided by a strong bond of friendship and mutual respect. Their household flourished on the foundation of love, trust, and unity, as they cherished each moment together with gratitude and affection.

Revanth Reddy, the dedicated leader and future Chief Minister, possesses a unique set of hobbies that reflect his commitment to public service and his passion for staying informed. His evenings are often spent engrossed in watching news channels, diligently taking notes on key points to later articulate in the assembly or in front of the public. This practice extends into the late hours of the night, sometimes with the assistance of his supportive wife who joins him in this endeavour.

However, before assuming the role of chief minister, Revanth Reddy indulged in a more leisurely pursuit: watching movies. He fondly recalls the simple pleasure of enjoying a movie, often accompanied by his favourite dish, biryani. Yet, amidst his busy schedule, he prioritizes quality time with his beloved daughter, Nymisha. Together, they share moments of joy attending movies and exploring various places, nurturing their bond as father and daughter.

Acknowledgements

Path of Inspiration

Revanth Reddy, a leader who rose from humble beginnings to great heights with sheer determination. With courage that overcame obstacles, he showcased exemplary leadership that brought light to Telangana. Earning the admiration of the people, guiding the way for social justice, strengthening bonds with rural communities, and paving the path for a new Telangana, he became a beacon of change.

Revanth Reddy's leadership stands for service, with the welfare of the people as its primary goal. He faced challenges head-on, stood strong, and became a pillar of support for transformation. Upholding his values with integrity, he emerged as a beacon of hope for Telangana. Revanth Reddy's life serves as a remarkable example of achieving greatness through persistence. The steps he took for the welfare of the people convey the profound messages of a true leader's life.

Konda Murali, Author

9441431090

Prologue

My name is Konda Murali,
In poetry, I shine truly.
A teacher, poet, writer too,
Through words, I've fought and grew.
    Twenty books I've penned so far,
Each one tells just who we are.
With confidence, they all were made,
From life's lessons, none would fade.
    Composed sixteen hundred poems,
An encyclopedia of poetic signs.
The best, I hope, this land will see,
Where human emotions flow so free.
    With every thought, I've crafted rhyme,
A journey told in measured time.
    Konda Murali, Author
    9441434090

CHAPTER ONE

Overview of the political journey

Revanth Reddy played a pivotal role in shaping his journey towards becoming a prominent student leader, providing him with a solid foundation for his subsequent foray into politics. His involvement with ABVP further bolstered his political acumen and left an indelible mark on his career trajectory. Winning in the ZPTC elections served as a significant milestone, paving the way for his advancement in politics. His ability to inspire others with his eloquence garnered widespread admiration and instilled confidence in his leadership abilities.

Upon entering politics, he displayed unwavering determination, never allowing obstacles to deter his path forward. Despite encountering numerous challenges along the way, he remained steadfast in his commitment to achieving success. His resilience in the face of adversity became a hallmark of his political journey, propelling him towards greater accomplishments.

Shortly after his triumph in the ZPTC elections, within a remarkably short span of time, Revanth Reddy seized the opportunity to contest in the MLC elections representing local bodies in undivided Andhra Pradesh. Once again, he embarked on his political journey as an independent candidate, demonstrating his confidence and determination. The outcome proved astounding as Reddy emerged victorious in the MLC elections, defeating the candidate from the Congress party. This resounding win captured the attention of the entire state, catapulting Revanth Reddy into the limelight of political prominence. His sudden rise to stardom in the realm of politics was undeniable, marking a significant milestone in his burgeoning career.

Revanth Reddy's victory in the MLC elections drew the attention of both print and electronic media, sparking curiosity among the public. People were pleasantly surprised by his articulate manner of speaking and his deep understanding of societal issues. In a remarkably short period, his name became synonymous with political discourse across the state. As news of his success spread, numerous political parties sought to court him, recognizing the potential he brought as an independent candidate. However, amidst this newfound attention, Reddy found himself grappling with a dilemma: determining which political party would best align with his goals and aspirations.

Revanth Reddy, considering his family ties to the Congress through his uncle, the notable politician Jaipal Reddy, initially contemplated joining the Congress party. However, recognizing the need to strategically align himself with a party that would best serve his interests, he weighed his options carefully. Ultimately, it was the welcoming gesture of Nara Chandrababu Naidu, the President of the Telugu Desam Party (TDP), that swayed Reddy's decision. After much deliberation, Revanth Reddy made the pivotal choice to join the TDP, believing it to be the most advantageous move given his circumstances. This decision proved instrumental in significantly bolstering his political stature and influence.

During a critical juncture when other political parties criticized the Telugu Desam Party (TDP) for its reluctance to express support for the separate statehood of Telangana by writing to the Central Government, he, despite being affiliated with the TDP, exerted pressure on Nara Chandrababu Naidu to draft and dispatch the necessary correspondence. Eventually, the letter was successfully dispatched to the Central Government, validating his stance on the imperative need for the formation of Telangana.

Revanth Reddy, a prominent political figure, earned the trust of the people in the Kodangal constituency by winning the MLA seat twice, first in 2009 and then again in 2014. The latter victory coincided with a significant event in Telangana's history—the formation of the Telangana State in 2014.

The Telangana Rashtra Samithi (TRS) party, spearheaded by K. Chandrashekar Rao (KCR), played a pivotal role in the formation of Telangana. The public's respect for the TRS party led to KCR assuming the position of Chief Minister. However, KCR's approach after assuming power raised eyebrows, particularly his tactic of luring MLAs from other parties into the TRS fold, notably targeting members of the Telugu Desam Party (TDP).

KCR's objective was clear, to weaken and eventually eliminate the TDP's presence in Telangana politics. In response to KCR's tactics, Revanth Reddy emerged as a vocal critic of the TRS government, standing firm against its policies and decisions. Despite facing pressure and attempts to discredit him, Revanth Reddy remained resolute and unyielding.

As the lone voice against the TRS juggernaut and with little support from within his own party, Revanth Reddy found himself in a challenging position. Eventually, in 2017, he made the decision to join the Congress party, marking the beginning of his affiliation with the party.

Through his courageous stance and unwavering commitment to his principles, Revanth Reddy has become a symbol of opposition against the TRS government's strategies and a key figure in Telangana's political landscape.

CHAPTER TWO

Visionary Thinking

Revanth Reddy's vision for Telangana represents a comprehensive and forward-thinking approach to governance, aiming to transform the state into a model of development, prosperity, and sustainability. His blueprint for the future is not just about addressing the immediate challenges but also about laying a strong foundation for long-term growth and well-being.

Central to Revanth Reddy's vision is the ambition to make Telangana a developed state, free from the burden of debt. This goal is crucial for ensuring that the state can pursue its developmental agenda without the constraints of financial liabilities. Achieving economic prosperity requires prudent fiscal management, efficient resource allocation, and robust economic planning. Revanth Reddy's approach involves creating a self sustaining economy that does not rely on external borrowing but instead harness the state's resources to fuel growth. By focussing on financial stability, Telangana can invest more in infrastructure, education, healthcare, and other critical sectors, leading to sustainable development that benefits all citizens.

Farmers are the backbone of Telangana's economy, and Revanth Reddy's vision places their well being at the forefront. He recognizes that for the state to prosper, its farmers must be happy and thriving. His vision includes implementing policies that ensure fair prices for crops, access to modern agricultural techniques, and support during natural calamities. By creating an environment where farmers are self-sufficient and prosperous, Revanth Reddy aims to build a strong agricultural foundation that contributes to overall economic growth. This approach not only secures the livelihoods of farmers but also ensures food security for the entire state.

In today's world, environmental sustainability is no longer an option but a necessity. Revanth Reddy envisions a Telangana where development goes hand in hand with environmental preservation. His vision includes promoting green technologies, conserving natural resources, and ensuring that development projects do not harm the environment. By fostering a balance between growth and ecological preservation, Revanth Reddy aims to safeguard Telangana's natural heritage for future generations. This commitment to sustainability reflects a forward-thinking approach that acknowledges the importance of protecting the environment while pursuing economic development.

Education is the cornerstone of Revanth Reddy's vision for Telangana. He aspires to achieve full literacy by enhancing the state's educational infrastructure and ensuring the quality education for all. This involves building and upgrading schools, providing necessary resources, and training teachers to deliver the best possible education. Revanth Reddy understands that a literate and educated population is more likely to contribute positively to the state's development and embrace progressive changes. By prioritizing education, he aims to empower the youth of Telangana, equipping them with the knowledge and skills needed to drive the state's future growth,

Healthcare is a fundamental right, and Revanth Reddy's vision includes providing comprehensive health facilities to every citizen of Telangana. He envisions a state where no one is denied access to quality healthcare, regardless of their socio-economic status. This includes establishing hospitals, clinics, and healthcare programs across the state, with a particular focus on rural and unreserved areas. In addition to healthcare, Revanth Reddy's vision encompasses the provision of basic amenities such as clean water, sanitation and electricity. These are essential for improving living standards and fostering a healthier society. By addressing these basic needs, Revanth Reddy aims to create a state where every citizen can live with dignity and security.

Revanth Reddy places great emphasis on financial prudence, with a focus on saving funds for future generations. He understands that sustainable development requires careful financial management, with investments made in long-term projects that benefit the state in years to come. By creating financial reserves, Telangana can ensure that future generations inherit a stable and prosperous state. This approach reflects a deep sense of responsibility towards the future, ensuring that the state is prepared to face any economic challenges that may arise.

Adherence to constitutional rule and the establishment of a drug-free state are pivotal elements of Revanth Reddy's vision. He believes that upholding the principles of democracy, justice, and equality is essential for ensuring fair governance and the rule of law. By ensuring that the government operates within the framework of the constitution, Revanth Reddy aims to build a state that respects the rights and freedoms of all its citizens. Additionally, his commitment to creating a drug-free state reflects his dedication to public health and safety. By implementing stringent measures to combat drug abuse, he aims to create a healthier and safer society, free from the scourge of addiction.

Employment generation is a key component of Revanth Reddy's vision for Telangana. He envisions a state where every individual has access to gainful employment, thereby reducing poverty and improving quality of life. This includes creating jobs in various sectors, from agriculture and industry to services and technology. In addition to employment, his vision includes the enhancements of irrigation facilities, which are crucial for agricultural development. By ensuring that farmers have adequate water supply, the state can boost agricultural productivity and ensure food security. These initiatives are critical for driving economic growth and improving the livelihoods of Telangana's citizens.

Revanth Reddy's vision for Telangana is a holistic and inclusive blueprint for the state's future. By focussing on economic stability, farmer welfare, environmental sustainability, education, healthcare, financial prudence, constitutional governance, and employment, he aims to build a Telangana that is prosperous, sustainable, and equitable. His vision is one that seeks to uplift every citizen, ensuring that no one is left behind. If realized, this vision promotes a bright future for Telangana, where development is balanced with sustainability, and every citizen has the opportunity to thrive. Revanth Reddy's leadership, guided by this vision, has the potential to transform Telangana into a symbol of hope of progress and prosperity in India.

Decision Making Skills

Revanth Reddy's decision-making skills at every stage of his life have been exemplary. It is his strategic decisions that ultimately led him to the position of Chief Minister. From winning the ZPTC election to ascending to the Chief Minister's office, every choice he made was remarkable. Strong decision-making, combined with excellent soft skills, is essential for achieving such success.

Revanth Reddy's political trajectory has been marked by a series of significant milestones and opportunities. In 2006, he made his debut in local politics by securing a victory as a Zilla Parishad Territorial Constituency (ZPTC) member, running as an independent candidate. The following year, in 2007, he further solidified his position by successfully contesting as an independent candidate in the Member of Legislative Council (MLC) elections from Kodangal. However, recognizing the potential for growth and influence within a political party, he made the strategic decision to join the Telugu Desam Party (TDP) in 2008. His association with the TDP proved fruitful, as evidenced by his resounding victory in the 2009 general elections, where he secured a landslide win as the Member of the Legislative Assembly (MLA) from the Kodangal constituency, garnering widespread support and trust from the electorate. This series of accomplishments and transitions underscored Revanth Reddy's emergence as a formidable force in Andhra Pradesh's political landscape.

In 2017, he parted ways with the TDP and joined the Indian National Congress party, marking a new chapter in his political journey. The following year, in 2018, he faced a setback when he lost the Telangana Legislative Assembly election from the Kodangal constituency as a Congress party candidate.

However, Revanth Reddy's resilience shone through in 2019 when he was elected to the Lok Sabha from the Malkajgiri Constituency as a Congress party candidate, reaffirming his popularity and support among the electorate.

In 2021, his leadership qualities were recognized when he was appointed as the president of the Telangana Pradesh Congress Committee (TPCC), further solidifying his position within the party.

The pinnacle of his political career came in 2023 when he was elected as an MLA from the Kodangal constituency. Notably, he made history by becoming the second Chief Minister of Telangana and the first Chief Minister from the Congress party, showcasing his evolution from a grassroots politician to a prominent leader in the state.

The process of electing a Chief Minister within the Congress Party is typically intricate due to the presence of numerous senior members, necessitating extensive discussions. However, Revanth Reddy's ascent to the position was remarkably smooth, facilitated by his instrumental role in thrusting the party back into the limelight after a decade-long hiatus. His undeniable charisma played a pivotal role in securing victory for the party in Telangana, effectively rejuvenating its fortunes.

Recognizing his contributions, the party's high command swiftly endorsed his candidacy, acknowledging his ability to deliver success for the party during critical junctures.

Revanth Reddy's decision-making skills were evident when he became the TPCC Chief. Despite initial dissatisfaction among many Congress leaders with the party's high command and slanders from his own party members, he used his leadership skills to unite the party before the elections. His ability to assess different options effectively and confidently is a hallmark of great leadership. Revanth Reddy thoroughly understands issues, gathers relevant information, and, with his analytical thinking, collaborates with others to make informed decisions. Problem-solving has become second nature to him, showcasing his capability as a dynamic leader.

His revolutionary decisions include the establishment of the Mother Telangana statue, which represents a typical Telangana woman, the creation of 50,000 government jobs, the formation of HYDRA (Hyderabad Disaster Response and Asset Monitoring Agency), and the ambitious River Musi Renaissance project. These initiatives reflect his vision and dedication to the state's development and cultural heritage.

CHAPTER FOUR

Crisis Management

When Reddy faces unexpected challenges, he handles them with remarkable cleverness and composure. Despite experiencing a few setbacks in his political career, he consistently turns them into opportunities. For instance, after losing the M.L.A seat in the 2018 Assembly elections in Kodangal, he bounced back with an impressive victory as an M.P in the 2019 Parliament elections. His resilience and ability to adapt showcase his exceptional leadership qualities.

Revanth Reddy demonstrates a steadfast commitment to upholding the rule of law and ensuring accountability in matters concerning government land. With a keen sense of justice, he is prepared to take decisive action against individuals who unlawfully lay claim to government-owned land. His deep understanding of land policies enables him to identify and thwart attempts to deceive the government, safeguarding public resources from exploitation and abuse.

Recognizing the prevalence of corruption and malpractice among certain politicians, he advocates for the need for counselling and reform within the political sphere. He believes that addressing the root causes of unethical behaviour is essential for fostering a culture of integrity and accountability in governance.

At the core of his mission is the pursuit of social justice. He tirelessly endeavours to address systemic inequalities and injustices, working towards creating a society where all individuals are treated fairly and equitably. Through his unwavering dedication to ethical governance and his commitment to upholding the principles of justice and fairness, Revanth Reddy emerges as a beacon of hope for those who seek a more just and equitable society.

Revanth Reddy's deep understanding of water policies enables him to effectively manage the state's share of water resources, ensuring that farmers receive the support they need to thrive. By prioritizing the equitable distribution of water, he works tirelessly to ensure that farmers benefit from reliable access to this vital resource, thereby enhancing agricultural productivity and livelihoods across the state.

However, Revanth is not afraid to speak out against wasteful government spending, particularly in large-scale projects such as the Kaleshwaram project. He has publicly criticized the misuse of funds allocated to this project, highlighting how it has become a symbol of excess and inefficiency under previous administrations. He contends that the project has been treated like an "ATM" by the government, squandering valuable resources that could be better utilized for the benefit of the people.

Moreover, Revanth is a staunch advocate for democratic principles and vehemently opposes the perpetuation of familial rule in politics. He endeavors to establish a truly democratic system of governance that empowers all citizens and ensures accountability, transparency, and fair representation in decision-making processes. Through his vocal criticism of government mismanagement and his unwavering commitment to democratic ideals, Revanth

Reddy emerges as a champion for the people, fighting tirelessly to uphold their rights and interests.

The creation of Telangana was driven by the aspirations for better access to funds, water resources, and job opportunities. However, since its establishment, these promises have been neglected, leading to frustration and disappointment among the people. Revanth Reddy, known for his outspokenness, has been particularly critical of the government's failure to conduct TSPSC exams properly, resulting in the neglect of unemployed individuals who rely on these exams for employment opportunities.

Furthermore, there has been a perceived decline in the importance placed on universities under the BRS government, exacerbating the challenges faced by students and academics alike. Upon assuming power, Revanth Reddy wasted no time in addressing these concerns. He swiftly issued appointment orders to Gurukula Teachers and ensured the prompt release of notifications for DSC and group exams, demonstrating his commitment to prioritizing the needs of the unemployed population. Through his actions, Revanth Reddy seeks to restore faith in the government's ability to address the pressing issues of unemployment and educational access, ultimately striving to create a more equitable and prosperous future for all residents of Telangana.

Public Speaking and Mass Appeal

Revanth Reddy possesses remarkable qualities and skills, with his public speaking ability standing out as the most significant. His speeches resonate with people, striking their minds like a bullet. This exceptional oratory skill has cemented his position as a substitute leader in Telangana. The people of Telangana believe that Revanth Reddy has the power to influence and govern effectively. His speeches consistently attract a distinct and widespread audience, amplifying his mass appeal.

Historically, great orators like Martin Luther King Jr. and Swami Vivekananda delivered their speeches with meticulous preparation and planning. They understood their audiences, maintained eye contact, used meaningful gestures, and employed proper voice modulation. Similarly, Revanth Reddy delivers impactful speeches, whether in casual contexts or large public gatherings. Before speaking, he thoroughly collects rebuttal information, ensuring his arguments are robust and well-informed.

Through his eloquence, Revanth Reddy effectively conveys the messages he wishes to share with the public. This skill has played a pivotal role in his emergence as a great leader. The diction in his speeches is particularly significant, as it sets the tone, style, and meaning of his messages. For instance, his discourse on the Kaleshwaram project successfully reached the public, thanks to his exceptional oratory skills.

Born in Mahabubnagar, Revanth Reddy's dialect carries a unique charm that resonates with the people of Telangana. His natural way of speaking enhances his connection with the audience, making him a relatable and influential figure in the region.

Revanth Reddy is renowned for his dynamic and persuasive public speaking skills, which have significantly contributed to his political success. One of the key aspects of his speaking style is his charismatic delivery. With a commanding stage presence, Revanth speaks with passion and conviction, which naturally captivates his audience and draws them into his message. This ability to command attention allows him to make a strong impact during his speeches.

Another important feature of his public speaking is the clarity and simplicity of his message. Revanth ensures that his speeches are clear, direct, and easy to understand, allowing him to effectively communicate with people from various backgrounds and demographics. His straightforward approach makes complex issues more relatable, which resonates with a wide audience.

Humour and wit are also essential elements of Revanth's speaking style. He often includes witty remarks and humorous anecdotes in his speeches, creating a sense of connection with his audience. This light-hearted touch helps to maintain engagement and makes his speeches more memorable. At the same time, he uses emotional appeal to tap into the feelings of his listeners. Revanth addresses issues that matter most to the people, presenting himself as a leader who understands their concerns, which strengthens his bond with the masses.

In addition to emotional appeal, Revanth Reddy incorporates fact-based arguments into his speeches. He combines emotion with well-researched facts, which lend credibility to his words. This balance of emotion and logic makes his speeches powerful and persuasive, enabling him to effectively communicate his ideas and vision.

Fluency in both Telugu, Hindi and English allows Revanth to connect with a diverse range of audiences. Whether he is speaking to rural communities or urban intellectuals, his language proficiency ensures that his message reaches people across Telangana and beyond. Furthermore, his adaptability as a speaker is remarkable; he tailors his speeches to suit the occasion, audience, and context, making his words more relevant and impactful in different settings.

Lastly, Revanth Reddy's confidence and assertiveness are evident in his speeches. His assertive tone not only highlights his leadership qualities but also inspires trust in his vision. The confidence with which he addresses his audience establishes him as a strong, decisive leader, further cementing his position as a key figure in Telangana politics.

These public speaking skills have been instrumental in helping Revanth Reddy connect with the masses, build his reputation, and establish himself as a significant political leader.

CHAPTER SIX

Media Relations

Revanth Reddy has established a strong and strategic relationship with the media, which has played a pivotal role in shaping his political career and public image. His active engagement with the media allows him to reach a broader audience, where he frequently shares his opinions, clarifies his position on various issues, and addresses any controversies that may arise. Whether through press conferences, interviews, or debates, he ensures his voice is heard, creating an effective platform to communicate directly with the public. This active participation enables him to maintain visibility and ensure that his viewpoints are communicated clearly and effectively.

One of the key aspects of Revanth's media strategy is his transparency. Known for his straightforwardness, he garners the trust of both journalists and the public. His willingness to address tough questions head-on demonstrates his openness and confidence, which not only enhances his credibility but also establishes him as a leader who is unafraid to confront challenges directly. This transparency fosters trust, and as a result, he is able to maintain a strong and consistent narrative in the media.

Revanth has also proven himself adept at crisis management, especially when political challenges or controversies arise. He handles these situations with a level-headed approach, providing timely clarifications and controlling the narrative to his advantage. His ability to manage potential setbacks and turn them into opportunities further reinforces his position as a resilient leader, able to navigate difficult situations with strategic communication.

In addition to traditional media, Revanth Reddy has successfully embraced the power of social media. Actively using platforms such as Twitter, Facebook, and Instagram, he directly connects with citizens, shares updates, and rallies support. His social media presence amplifies his reach, allowing him to disseminate messages quickly and engage with the masses in real-time. This modern approach to communication has significantly bolstered his visibility and political relevance, especially among younger demographics who rely heavily on digital platforms for news and updates.

Revanth understands the importance of maintaining positive relationships with journalists and media houses. By fostering these connections, he ensures balanced coverage and effective dissemination of his ideas and viewpoints. His regular interaction with both regional and national media outlets allows him to keep his presence felt in the political discourse, ensuring that his perspectives remain relevant and visible in public discussions.

Leveraging media to advocate for public causes is another key element of Revanth's media relations strategy. He uses media platforms not just to promote his own political agenda but also to highlight issues that affect the public. By criticizing ineffective policies and drawing attention to problems that matter to the people, he positions himself as a leader who is genuinely concerned about public welfare, aligning himself with the interests of the common people.

Revanth's charismatic persona further enhances his media presence. His confidence and articulate speeches make headlines, increasing his visibility and ensuring that his messages are heard loud and clear. This magnetic presence makes him a compelling figure in political debates, drawing attention to his ideas and strengthening his position as a leader with a distinct voice in the political arena.

Finally, Revanth Reddy uses the media as a platform to challenge opposition parties and expose their shortcomings. Whether through direct confrontations or strategic critiques, he makes use of media outlets to present his viewpoints while also highlighting the failures of his political rivals.

CHAPTER SEVEN

Interpersonal Communication

Revanth Reddy's interpersonal communication skills have played a crucial role in his rise as a prominent political leader in Telangana. His ability to connect with people from all walks of life, ranging from grassroots workers to political leaders and the general public, has been one of his greatest assets. One of the most significant qualities that define his communication style is his empathy and approachability. Revanth's ability to make people feel comfortable and heard has been key to building trust and rapport. He listens actively, engaging with others in a way that ensures they feel valued and understood, which fosters strong relationships and encourages open communication.

Coming from a rural background himself, Revanth has a natural ability to relate to the struggles and aspirations of ordinary citizens, particularly farmers and marginalized groups. His personal experiences resonate deeply with the people he interacts with, allowing him to connect on a more personal level. This reliability makes his messages more impactful, as the people he communicates with often see him as one of their own, someone who understands their challenges and can advocate for their interests.

In addition to his empathetic nature, Revanth Reddy excels in persuasive communication. He has a remarkable ability to convince others of his vision and ideas, whether he is motivating his party workers or negotiating with political allies. His arguments are always grounded in facts and delivered with conviction, making them compelling and effective. This persuasive skill has enabled him to rally support and build consensus among diverse groups, further strengthening his position as a leader.

Building personal relationships is another key strength of Revanth's communication. He takes the time to invest in long-term relationships with his colleagues, party members, and community leaders. This focus on personal connections reflects his trustworthiness and dedication, which have helped him maintain strong ties within his political network. His ability to sustain these relationships over time has contributed significantly to his success in the political arena.

Revanth also demonstrates exceptional skills in conflict resolution, a vital aspect of interpersonal communication. In the often complex and contentious world of politics, he is adept at resolving disputes within his party and among different groups. His diplomatic approach allows him to facilitate open communication, encouraging dialogue and finding common ground. This ability to address disagreements constructively has helped him navigate challenging political landscapes and maintain stability within his team.

One of the remarkable aspects of Revanth Reddy's communication is his adaptability. He is able to tailor his communication style to suit various audiences, whether he is addressing rural communities, engaging with urban intellectuals, or debating with political rivals. This flexibility enhances his effectiveness in diverse settings, allowing him to connect with people from different backgrounds and interests.

As a leader, Revanth inspires and motivates his team through clear and consistent communication. He communicates a compelling vision for the future and ensures his team understands their roles in achieving that vision. His ability to delegate responsibilities while maintaining unity within the team further reflects his strong leadership qualities. He motivates his supporters by recognizing their contributions and creating a sense of purpose within the group.

Revanth's assertiveness is another key trait in his communication style. He ensures that his points are heard, but he does so in a manner that is respectful of others. His assertive yet respectful communication fosters an environment where ideas can be discussed openly, and different perspectives are valued. This approach helps him maintain credibility and authority while promoting cooperation and mutual respect.

Finally, Revanth's charismatic presence adds another layer of strength to his communication. His energy and enthusiasm make his interactions engaging and memorable, leaving a lasting impression on those he speaks to. This charismatic demeanour enhances his ability to inspire and rally support, further solidifying his position as a leader who can captivate and unite people.

Overall, Revanth Reddy's interpersonal communication skills have been essential to his political success. His ability to connect with people on a personal level, build strong relationships, resolve conflicts, and motivate others has enabled him to effectively manage his political party and gain widespread support. These communication skills continue to play a pivotal role in his leadership, making him a highly respected and influential figure in Telangana politics.

CHAPTER EIGHT

Electoral Strategies

Revanth Reddy's rise as a prominent political leader in Telangana can be attributed to his dynamic approach to electoral strategies. His emphasis on grassroots mobilization has been instrumental in building a strong connection with the electorate. By directly engaging with farmers, youth, women, and marginalized communities, he has been able to understand and address their concerns effectively. This connection fosters trust and ensures that his leadership resonates with the people.

A significant aspect of Revanth's approach is his focus on issue-based campaigning. He prioritizes matters that deeply affect the public, such as unemployment, farmer welfare, corruption, and infrastructure development. His campaigns often highlight the shortcomings of the ruling government while presenting actionable solutions. This approach not only exposes governance failures but also positions him as a leader with practical ideas for change.

Strategic alliances form another cornerstone of Revanth's electoral success. By building relationships with influential leaders and community representatives, he consolidates support in key constituencies. These alliances strengthen his position and widen his reach among diverse voter groups. Furthermore, his strong critique of the ruling

Bharatha Rashtra Samithi (BRS) amplifies his message. Through bold and outspoken criticism of governance failures and unfulfilled promises, Revanth captures media attention and directs the public discourse in his favour.

Revanth's ability to connect with younger voters has been remarkable, thanks to his effective use of social media platforms like Twitter, Facebook, and Instagram. His digital campaigns include live sessions, targeted posts, and engaging hash tags, ensuring his message reaches a broader audience. Complementing this modern approach is his commitment to personal interaction with voters. Through door-to-door campaigns, rallies, and town hall meetings, he fosters trust and builds a personal connection with the electorate.

One of Revanth's key strengths is his ability to craft compelling narratives. He portrays himself as a dynamic and people-centric leader, often emphasizing his journey from humble beginnings. This reliability endears him to voters and strengthens his appeal. In addition, he prioritizes the selection of candidates with strong local influence and clean reputations, ensuring they align with the aspirations of the voters in their constituencies.

As the president of the Telangana Pradesh Congress Committee (TPCC), Revanth ensures that the party machinery operates efficiently during elections. His coordination with party workers at all levels reflects his commitment to a unified campaign strategy. He also balances his focus on both rural and urban issues, addressing farmer distress and irrigation needs alongside urban challenges like infrastructure and employment. This comprehensive approach ensures his appeal across different segments of the population.

Revanth's charismatic leadership plays a vital role in his electoral success. His energetic and fearless persona attracts voters, particularly those seeking a leader who can challenge the status quo. Additionally, he participates in symbolic gestures such as protests and padyatras, showcasing his dedication to public causes and reinforcing his connection with the masses.

Through a strategic blend of grassroots engagement, issue-driven campaigns, modern outreach techniques, and effective leadership, Revanth Reddy has established himself as a formidable figure in Telangana politics. His ability to connect with the electorate, address their concerns, and inspire confidence in his vision for the future continues to make him a key player in the political landscape.

CHAPTER NINE

Policy Implementation

Revanth Reddy, as the Chief Minister of Telangana, has played a pivotal role in advocating for transformative policies, influencing governance, and shaping public discourse to address the pressing needs of the state. His leadership reflects a deep commitment to creating a more equitable and progressive Telangana, with a focus on comprehensive development across sectors.

A cornerstone of his governance has been his unwavering advocacy for farmer welfare. Revanth has consistently emphasized the importance of farmer-friendly policies, including loan waivers, better Minimum Support Prices (MSP), and the implementation of efficient irrigation projects. By raising concerns about delays in programs like the Rythu Bharosa scheme and demanding greater accountability in agricultural support, he has ensured that the voices of farmers are heard and addressed at the policy level.

Employment generation has been another significant area of focus under Revanth's leadership. He has been a vocal critic of the failure to fill previous government vacancies and has proposed reforms to enhance transparency and efficiency in recruitment processes. His dedication to creating more jobs, particularly for the youth, demonstrates his commitment to tackling one of the state's most pressing challenges. Within one year he could give 50,000 government jobs through TGSPSC and other recruitments boards.

In the sectors of education and health, Revanth has consistently called for increased investment in government schools, colleges, and hospitals. His policies aim to improve the quality of education, ensure access to free healthcare, and upgrade infrastructure in both rural and urban areas. By prioritizing these fundamental sectors, he seeks to address long-standing inequalities and create opportunities for all citizens. Integrated Gurukulas in each assembly constituency is initiated. The core idea behind it is to ensure healthy and conducive learning atmosphere by constructing permanent buildings.

Transparency and anti-corruption measures have been central to Revanth's governance. He has exposed alleged irregularities in large-scale projects such as the Kaleshwaram Lift Irrigation Scheme, calling for audits and accountability. His efforts to implement stricter anti-corruption policies underscore his commitment to fostering a governance model rooted in integrity and fairness.

Revanth has also been a staunch advocate for the welfare of marginalized communities, including Dalits, tribals, and backward classes. His policies are aimed at improving their socio-economic conditions through schemes for housing, education, and financial inclusion. By addressing the needs of these communities, he has worked to bridge social and economic divides, ensuring that no section of society is left behind.

Environmental sustainability has been another critical area of focus. Revanth has raised concerns about environmental degradation and the ineffective execution of programs like Haritha Haram, Telangana's Afforestation initiative. He has advocated for policies that promote sustainable development and stricter measures to protect natural resources, such as lakes and forests, ensuring a balance between development and environmental preservation. One of it is HYDRA. HYDRA stands as a guardian for the lakes of the city, a fierce opponent to those who seek to grab land unlawfully. It targets illegal constructions and actively fights against encroachments, upholding justice and protecting natural resources.

One of its key missions is to cleanse the polluted Musi River and mitigate the risks of flooding. By lighting up the city streets and ensuring safer urban spaces, HYDRA has become a boon for the residents, bringing hope and order. Much like a fearless warrior, HYDRA wields its power against encroachments, acting as a weapon of justice and a saviour of democracy. It feels like divine intervention, offering strength and solutions during challenging times.

Unstoppable in its efforts, HYDRA spreads its influence far and wide, aiming to preserve the tranquillity of nature. It serves as a protective shield for the dreams of the people and safeguards the invaluable assets of the capital city. With the relentless force of ocean waves and the radiance of divine light, HYDRA has emerged as a shining example of effective urban governance, symbolizing hope and resilience in this era.

Another policy that has been initiated is the Musi Riverfront Development Project. It is a flagship initiative to rejuvenate Hyderabad's iconic river. Inspired by global riverfront projects like London's Thames and India's Sabarmati Riverfront, the project aims to transform the Musi River into a vibrant hub for tourism, business, and culture.

The initiative focuses on improving living conditions, boosting livelihoods, enhancing environmental health, and promoting Hyderabad's global image. While addressing challenges like slums and poor infrastructure along the river, the government is ensuring fair compensation and housing for displaced families.

This transformative project is expected to bring far-reaching socio-economic benefits, much like similar successful riverfront developments in cities like Kota and Patna, and stands as a testament to Revanth Reddy's vision for a progressive and inclusive Telangana.

In urban areas, he has highlighted inefficiencies in infrastructure planning and implementation, particularly in Hyderabad. His vision for better policies regarding public transportation, roads, and water supply systems reflects his commitment to improving the quality of life for urban residents while addressing the challenges of rapid urbanization.

Empowerment of women has been another hallmark of his leadership. He has emphasized the importance of policies that ensure women's safety, education, and employment. His proposals to promote women entrepreneurs and create gender-sensitive work environments showcase his dedication to fostering a more inclusive society. To empower the women, Mahalakshmi Scheme is initiated immediately after he became the chief minister. The scheme provides free transport facilities to all the girls, women and transgender in Telangana.

As Chief Minister, Revanth Reddy has also demonstrated the importance of effective policy implementation. By working closely with Congress-ruled municipal bodies and local leaders, he has ensured that people-friendly policies are translated into actionable programs at the grassroots level. This collaborative approach reflects his vision for a participatory governance model that aligns with the aspirations of the people.

Through his leadership, Revanth Reddy has proven to be a dynamic and visionary leader committed to addressing the diverse needs of Telangana. His policy initiatives and governance style underscore his dedication to creating a state that is equitable, sustainable, and prosperous for all its citizens.

Grassroots Engagement

Revanth Reddy's political journey is deeply rooted in his active grassroots engagement, which has become a foundation stone of his strategy and leadership in Telangana. His ability to connect with the people, particularly the marginalized and underprivileged, has cemented his position as a leader who prioritizes the concerns of the common man. Through his relentless efforts to address local issues and empower communities, he has built a strong foundation of trust and support across the state.

Revanth's approach to grassroots engagement is characterized by his emphasis on direct interaction with the people. He frequently holds public meetings, town halls, and door-to-door campaigns, ensuring he remains accessible to citizens. This personal approach not only helps him understand their challenges but also allows him to build a bond of trust and transparency. By being present and attentive, he fosters a sense of belonging among the people, who see him as a leader genuinely invested in their welfare.

His focus on rural development has been another significant aspect of his grassroots efforts. Recognizing the pivotal role rural areas play in the state's overall progress, Revanth has championed initiatives to improve infrastructure, education, healthcare, and employment opportunities in these regions. He has worked tirelessly to bring development to the remotest corners of Telangana, ensuring that no community is left behind in the pursuit of progress.

Revanth's commitment to the empowerment of marginalized communities reflects his vision for a more inclusive society. He has been a staunch advocate for the rights of Dalits, backward classes, and other underprivileged groups, pushing for welfare schemes that provide education, employment, and social justice. His efforts have created opportunities for these communities to rise above systemic inequalities and participate more actively in the state's development.

In addition to structural reforms, Revanth has initiated several community welfare programs to address immediate local needs. These initiatives often focus on providing healthcare, scholarships, housing, and financial assistance to those in distress. By addressing these pressing concerns, he demonstrates a hands-on approach to leadership, ensuring that his efforts have a tangible and lasting impact on people's lives.

Farmers, a crucial segment of Telangana's population, have also been at the center of Revanth's grassroots engagement. He has consistently highlighted their struggles, advocating for fair prices for crops, better irrigation facilities, and timely financial aid to those facing distress. His dedication to farmers' welfare underscores his understanding of their critical role in the state's economy and the challenges they face in sustaining their livelihoods.

Revanth's connection with the youth of Telangana is another hallmark of his grassroots strategy. By engaging with young people through various programs and campaigns, he has encouraged them to take an active role in shaping the future of the state. His speeches often resonate with the aspirations of the younger generation, focusing on empowerment and inspiring them to contribute to social and political change.

Moreover, Revanth has prioritized inclusivity in decision-making processes, empowering local leaders and activists to take on larger roles in governance. By involving people at the grassroots level in shaping policies and initiatives, he has fostered a more democratic and participatory approach to leadership. This inclusivity not only strengthens the democratic fabric of Telangana but also ensures that governance reflects the voices and needs of the people.

Revanth Reddy's grassroots engagement is evidence to his deep commitment to the welfare of the people and his vision for a progressive and inclusive Telangana. His hands-on approach, focus on marginalized communities, and efforts to empower the youth and local leaders have created a strong connection with the citizens of the state. Through his work, he continues to inspire trust and hope, setting an example of how grassroots politics can drive meaningful change.

CHAPTER ELEVEN

Embracing Change

Revanth Reddy's journey is a remarkable tale of transformation and growth. From his modest beginnings in the heart of Telangana, he rose to prominence with unwavering determination. A leader deeply connected to the people, he faced numerous challenges but always embraced change, breaking free from outdated norms to usher in a new era of development.

Revanth Reddy made it possible to change Telangana Thalli which looks like ordinary Telangana woman. In the vibrant image of Telangana Thalli, her green saree embodies the natural beauty and agricultural richness of the state. She stands as a symbol of prosperity, exuding the fragrance of fertile lands. Her footsteps bring life to the fields, a testament to her unwavering spirit and confidence.

In one hand, she holds a sheaf of harvested crops, signifying her pride in agriculture and its cultural roots. As the mother of abundance, she stands tall as the guardian of Telangana's farming heritage, representing the hopes and aspirations of every farmer. Her gaze is fixed firmly on the future, illuminating the path of progress. With a strong heart and resilient dreams, she reflects the purpose and determination etched into the lives of the people. Her blessings nurture green fields, while her vision paves the way for sustainable growth.

Telangana Thalli, the architect of a greener Telangana, holds within her hands the light of prosperity. She is the eternal symbol of hope and progress, guiding her children toward a brighter world. Forever an inspiration, Telangana Thalli embodies the pride of the state, a beacon of resilience, and a harbinger of development, uniting her people with dreams of shared success and growth.

With a vision to elevate his state, Revanth Reddy answered the call for progress, focusing on welfare and justice for all. His leadership extended from rural villages to bustling cities, where his dream of a better future for Telangana took shape. His policies, aimed at strengthening the weaker sections of society, were a testament to his unique and bold approach.

Through every obstacle, he saw opportunity rather than setback. His belief in the power of change was evident in his tireless efforts for reform, ensuring that his people were uplifted through unity and commitment. Embracing change was not just a strategy for him but a guiding principle. With his visionary leadership, he consistently worked toward making Telangana a beacon of progress, standing as a true example of what can be achieved when one embraces change with courage and purpose.

Technological Awareness

Revanth Reddy's political journey reflects a forward-thinking approach that emphasizes technological integration in governance and development. His tenure as Chief Minister of Telangana showcases a deep understanding of how technology can transform governance, enhance infrastructure, and improve the quality of life for citizens. By focusing on modernization and innovation, he has made significant strides in shaping a technologically advanced and inclusive state.

A key aspect of his leadership has been the promotion of smart city initiatives. Revanth has prioritized the modernization of urban infrastructure through the adoption of smart technologies, such as the Internet of Things (IoT). These advancements have contributed to better city planning, improved traffic management, and effective environmental monitoring. Under his guidance, cities in Telangana are evolving into hubs of efficiency and sustainability, setting benchmarks for urban development across the country.

Revanth's commitment to technology is also evident in his advocacy for digital governance. By supporting the digitalization of government services, he has streamlined administrative processes, making them more transparent and accessible. E-governance initiatives introduced under his leadership have empowered citizens by reducing bureaucratic hurdles and ensuring the efficient delivery of services. These efforts underscore his vision of a government that is both accountable and citizen-centric.

In the realm of education, Revanth has demonstrated an acute awareness of the importance of equipping the younger generation with the skills required to thrive in modern job markets. He has emphasized the need for technical education and skill development programs, particularly in technology-driven sectors. By fostering an environment that promotes learning and innovation, he is preparing the youth of Telangana to excel in a competitive global economy.

Infrastructure development has been another cornerstone of Revanth's administration. His leadership has seen a focus on upgrading transportation systems and expanding digital infrastructure. Initiatives such as the introduction of eco-friendly e-buses and the promotion of Hyderabad as a technological hub through projects like T-Hub have reinforced Telangana's position as a leader in innovation and entrepreneurship. These efforts not only enhance urban mobility but also create opportunities for startups and tech enterprises to flourish.

Revanth's vision extends to the agricultural sector, where he has championed the use of modern technologies to improve productivity and support farmers. By promoting precision agriculture, drone technology for crop monitoring, and mobile applications that provide real-time data and expert guidance, he has revolutionized farming practices in the state. These technological interventions have empowered farmers with the tools and knowledge they need to make informed decisions, ensuring sustainable growth in the agrarian economy.

Environmental sustainability has also been a key focus area for Revanth Reddy. His administration has implemented smart water management systems that employ technology to reduce wastage and ensure efficient distribution. By addressing critical issues like water scarcity and resource mismanagement, he has demonstrated a commitment to preserving natural resources while meeting the needs of a growing population.

Revanth Reddy's technical awareness is a defining feature of his leadership, reflecting a comprehensive vision for the development of Telangana. His focus on modernization, digitalization, and technological innovation has not only advanced infrastructure and governance but also ensured that the benefits of these advancements reach every section of society. From urban centers to rural farmlands, his initiatives have created a balanced and inclusive approach to progress, positioning Telangana as a model state for technological excellence and sustainable growth.

CHAPTER THIRTEEN

Innovative Governance

Revanth Reddy, as the Chief Minister of Telangana, has emerged as a transformative leader, pioneering a governance model that prioritizes modernization, inclusivity, and sustainability. His innovative approach to administration reflects a deep understanding of the challenges faced by society and a commitment to addressing them through forward-thinking solutions. With a focus on citizen-centric governance, his leadership has introduced initiatives that enhance transparency, foster development, and create an equitable framework for progress.

A cornerstone of Revanth Reddy's administration is the digital transformation of governance. By integrating technology into public administration, he has ensured the swift and transparent delivery of essential services. E-governance platforms have been developed to streamline processes such as land registration, access to health schemes, and education services. These initiatives not only reduce bureaucratic inefficiencies but also empower citizens by making government services more accessible and reliable, thereby fostering trust in the system.

Urban development under Revanth Reddy's leadership has witnessed a remarkable shift towards sustainability and innovation. Projects like the Musi Riverfront Development exemplify his vision of combining urban renewal with environmental conservation. Inspired by globally recognized models, these initiatives leverage advanced urban planning and technological solutions to create sustainable ecosystems. Such projects not only enhance the quality of life for urban residents but also ensure the preservation of natural resources.

Agriculture, being the backbone of Telangana's economy, has received a significant boost through Revanth Reddy's innovative policies. By incorporating technology into farming practices, he has empowered farmers to enhance productivity and sustainability. Precision farming techniques, soil health monitoring through IoT, and real-time weather updates are among the measures introduced to modernize agriculture. These advancements provide farmers with the tools and information needed to make informed decisions, ensuring long-term growth and resilience in the sector.

Revanth Reddy's administration has also prioritized skill development and education to prepare the youth of Telangana for future challenges. By establishing coding schools in rural areas, forging partnerships with global technology companies, and setting up state-of-the-art training centers, he has bridged the gap between education and employability. These initiatives not only equip the younger generation with relevant skills but also contribute to the creation of a workforce that is competitive on a global scale.

Environmental consciousness is another hallmark of Revanth Reddy's governance. His commitment to sustainable development is evident in the introduction of renewable energy projects, smart water management systems, and the promotion of electric vehicle adoption. The rejuvenation of lakes and water bodies across Telangana further demonstrates his dedication to balancing progress with nature. These efforts ensure that economic growth is pursued without compromising the state's ecological integrity.

Decentralization of governance is a key aspect of Revanth Reddy's leadership philosophy. By empowering local self-governments and strengthening village and municipal councils, he has fostered a participatory approach to decision-making. This grassroots engagement ensures that policies are tailored to meet the specific needs of communities, thereby creating a more inclusive and effective governance model.

Revanth Reddy's welfare programs reflect his commitment to addressing the needs of marginalized communities. From introducing universal healthcare schemes to implementing affordable housing projects, his administration has prioritized inclusive growth. These initiatives are designed using data-driven approaches, ensuring that resources are allocated effectively and reach those who need them the most.

Economic growth through technological advancement has been another focal point of Revanth Reddy's governance. By promoting Hyderabad as a global IT hub, he has attracted significant investments and fostered innovation. Initiatives like T-Hub 2.0, which supports start-ups, and the integration of emerging technologies such as artificial intelligence and block chain into governance, have positioned Telangana as a tech-driven state with a dynamic economy.

Through his visionary leadership, Revanth Reddy has created a governance model that blends technology, sustainability, and inclusivity. His innovative initiatives address long-standing challenges with transformative solutions, setting a benchmark for modern leadership. By prioritizing the welfare of citizens, fostering economic growth, and ensuring environmental stewardship, Revanth Reddy's administration exemplifies a forward-looking approach to governance that paves the way for a brighter and more equitable future for Telangana.

CHAPTER FOURTEEN

Empathy and Compassion

Revanth Reddy, a leader known for his remarkable empathy and compassion, has established himself as a people's leader by consistently addressing the concerns of the underprivileged and marginalized. His deep understanding of societal struggles and genuine efforts to resolve them make him a beacon of hope for many.

Revanth Reddy's empathy is evident in his actions and words. He listens attentively to the grievances of farmers, labourers, and common citizens, ensuring their voices are heard and addressed. Whether it is advocating for farmer rights, fighting for equal opportunities for the youth, or standing up against injustice, he has consistently demonstrated a profound concern for societal well-being.

His compassion extends beyond politics into humanitarian efforts. During crises, such as natural disasters or economic hardships, Revanth Reddy has been at the forefront, organizing relief measures and offering aid to those in need. His ability to connect emotionally with people and understand their pain sets him apart as a leader who truly cares.

Unlike many leaders who merely promise change, Revanth Reddy ensures tangible outcomes. His initiatives often prioritize education, healthcare, and rural development, reflecting his commitment to uplifting the weaker sections of society. He believes that leadership is not about authority but about service, and his actions consistently embody this belief.

Through his compassionate approach, Revanth Reddy inspires others to take collective responsibility for the betterment of society. His leadership exemplifies the transformative power of empathy, proving that true progress can only be achieved by putting people first.

CHAPTER FIFTEEN

Conflict Resolution

Revanth Reddy has emerged as a leader adept at resolving conflicts, whether they stem from political disputes, societal issues, or community disagreements. His approach to conflict resolution is rooted in dialogue, transparency, and a commitment to justice, making him a trusted mediator in challenging situations.

One of his standout qualities is his ability to listen empathetically to all parties involved in a conflict. He ensures that every voice, no matter how marginalized, is heard and respected. By fostering open communication, he creates an environment where misunderstandings can be addressed, and mutual trust can be built.

Revanth Reddy also demonstrates a deep understanding of the complexities of conflicts. He approaches problems with a clear strategy, analyzing the root causes and proposing solutions that are both practical and fair. His ability to strike a balance between firmness and flexibility has often led to resolutions that satisfy all stakeholders.

In political conflicts, Revanth Reddy has shown remarkable courage and tact. He is not afraid to challenge the status quo or confront powerful adversaries when justice is at stake. At the same time, he prioritizes maintaining harmony and works towards peaceful solutions that benefit the larger community.

His conflict resolution skills extend beyond politics into social and community spheres. Whether it's addressing disputes over land, resources, or public policies, he has consistently acted as a bridge, bringing together diverse perspectives to achieve common goals.

Revanth Reddy's leadership in resolving conflicts reflects his vision of a united, progressive society. By prioritizing dialogue, fairness, and long-term solutions, he continues to inspire confidence and trust among the people he serves.

CHAPTER SIXTEEN

Team Building

Revanth Reddy is a leader renowned for his exceptional team-building abilities, which have been instrumental in his political journey and his vision for societal progress. His leadership style emphasizes collaboration, trust, and empowerment, enabling him to bring together diverse individuals to work toward common goals.

One of Revanth Reddy's strengths lies in identifying talent and nurturing it. He has a keen eye for recognizing potential and ensuring that his team members are positioned in roles that align with their strengths. This not only enhances efficiency but also fosters a sense of purpose and belonging among his team.

Revanth Reddy believes in leading by example, which inspires loyalty and dedication in his team. His work ethic, determination, and resilience motivate those around him to strive for excellence. He creates an environment where every team member feels valued and encouraged to contribute their ideas.

A hallmark of his team-building approach is open communication. Revanth Reddy ensures that his team operates transparently, with every member having a voice in decision-making processes. This inclusivity fosters trust and strengthens the bond within the team, making it more cohesive and effective.

In addition to fostering teamwork, Revanth Reddy is skilled at managing conflicts within his team. He encourages dialogue and mediates disputes with fairness and understanding, ensuring that differences do not hinder progress. His ability to resolve conflicts while maintaining harmony is a testament to his leadership acumen.

Through his team-building efforts, Revanth Reddy has created a network of committed individuals who share his vision for change. His ability to unite people from diverse backgrounds and guide them toward a shared purpose reflects his strength as a leader and his commitment to collective success.

CHAPTER SEVENTEEN

Building Alliances

Revanth Reddy, a dynamic leader and the Chief Minister of Telangana, showcased his political acumen and strategic vision through the successful alliance between the Congress Party and the Communist Party of India (CPI) during the Telangana Assembly elections. This partnership stands as a witness to his ability to transcend ideological differences and unite forces for a shared vision of progress and reform. In a political landscape marked by intense competition, Revanth Reddy's efforts to forge this alliance highlight his leadership qualities and commitment to democratic principles.

Faced with a formidable opponent in the Bharat Rashtra Samithi (BRS), Revanth Reddy recognized the need to consolidate opposition forces to present a strong challenge to the ruling establishment. The CPI, with its strong grassroots presence and significant influence among marginalized communities, became a key partner in this endeavour. Revanth's decision to approach the CPI reflected not only his political pragmatism but also his belief in the power of collective action to drive change.

The process of building this alliance required careful planning and skilful negotiation. Revanth Reddy initiated dialogues with CPI leaders by emphasizing common goals such as social justice, equitable development, and combating corruption. By focusing on shared values and objectives, he laid the foundation for a partnership built on trust and mutual respect. Transparent discussions and open communication were central to this process, ensuring that both parties felt heard and valued.

One of the critical aspects of this alliance was the allocation of constituencies, a process often fraught with potential conflicts in political collaborations. Revanth approached this task with sensitivity, addressing the CPI's aspirations while balancing Congress's broader electoral strategy. This careful handling of negotiations demonstrated his ability to navigate complex political dynamics while maintaining harmony within the alliance.

Once the partnership was formalized, Revanth Reddy led a unified campaign that highlighted the shared manifesto of the Congress-CPI coalition. This manifesto resonated with the aspirations of the people of Telangana, addressing issues such as inequality, corruption, and rural development. By presenting a cohesive vision for the state's future, the alliance successfully mobilized diverse voter bases and consolidated anti-incumbency sentiments against the ruling BRS.

The impact of this alliance was transformative, altering the political landscape of Telangana. The Congress-CPI coalition emerged as a formidable force, countering the dominance of the BRS and securing a decisive victory in the elections. This success not only paved the way for Revanth Reddy's ascent as Chief Minister but also demonstrated the potential of collaborative politics to drive meaningful change. The alliance's success was a reflection of Revanth's ability to unite diverse stakeholders under a common vision, ensuring that their combined efforts translated into tangible outcomes.

Revanth Reddy's approach to building alliances offers valuable lessons in political leadership. His inclusivity in accommodating the perspectives of all partners and his emphasis on clear and transparent communication fostered trust and cooperation. By grounding the alliance in a shared vision, he ensured that the partnership remained focused on its objectives, avoiding distractions or divisions. These principles underline the importance of collaboration in achieving not only electoral success but also broader societal transformation.

The Congress-CPI alliance, spearheaded by Revanth Reddy, stands as a powerful example of how political partnerships can transcend individual agendas to serve the greater good. His ability to navigate the complexities of coalition-building while maintaining focus on shared goals underscores his leadership and commitment to democratic values. Through this alliance, Revanth Reddy demonstrated that unity, guided by a clear and inclusive vision, can bring about profound change and pave the way for a brighter future for Telangana.

CHAPTER EIGHTEEN

Managing Political Relationships

Revanth Reddy, the Chief Minister of Telangana, has gained widespread recognition for his exceptional ability to manage complex political relationships. His approach combines strategic foresight, effective communication, and adaptability, which have enabled him to build alliances and strengthen his influence in Telangana's political landscape. His leadership reflects a deep understanding of human dynamics and political intricacies, which he skilfully navigates to foster trust and collaboration.

A characteristic of Revanth Reddy's political journey is his commitment to open communication. He prioritizes transparent dialogue with allies, opposition leaders, and party workers, creating an atmosphere of trust and cohesion. By fostering clear communication channels, he addresses conflicts and grievances promptly, ensuring that all stakeholders feel heard and valued. This approach has been instrumental in maintaining harmony within his party and strengthening his alliances.

His ability to forge strategic alliances further underscores his mastery of relationship management. His collaboration with the Communist Party of India (CPI) during the Telangana elections is a testament to his capacity to bring together diverse political ideologies for a common cause. By focusing on shared objectives such as social justice and development, he demonstrated how political relationships can be leveraged for mutual benefit. This alliance played a pivotal role in countering the dominance of the ruling party and securing electoral success for Congress.

Balancing internal and external dynamics is another key aspect of Revanth Reddy's leadership. Within his party, he has effectively managed dissent by addressing the concerns of party workers and ensuring inclusivity in decision-making. Externally, he has maintained a respectful yet competitive stance with opposing parties, demonstrating the ability to strike a delicate balance between rivalry and collaboration. This dual approach has earned him credibility and respect from both his peers and adversaries.

Revanth Reddy's emphasis on empowering grassroots leaders further highlights his inclusive leadership style. Recognizing the importance of local leadership, he ensures that grassroots leaders are actively involved in decision-making processes. This approach not only strengthens his relationships with party cadres but also broadens his influence among voters. By valuing the contributions of local leaders, he fosters a sense of ownership and loyalty within his political network.

Flexibility and adaptability are central to Revanth Reddy's success in managing political relationships. He adjusts his strategies to align with changing political scenarios, demonstrating the ability to negotiate and compromise without sacrificing his core values. This pragmatic approach allows him to navigate challenges effectively while maintaining focus on long-term goals.

At the heart of his leadership is a focus on a shared vision for progress and development. Whether his party or in alliances, he emphasizes the importance of collective goals that unite diverse stakeholders. This focus on a common purpose creates a sense of direction and reinforces the bonds between political partners.

The impact of Revanth Reddy's relationship management is evident in the strengthened alliances he has forged. His efforts have enabled Congress to form strong coalitions, such as the CPI alliance, which proved instrumental in achieving electoral victories. His ability to navigate political dynamics has also enhanced his credibility, earning him the trust of party members and voters alike. Furthermore, his skill in managing relationships has solidified his reputation as an inclusive and forward-thinking leader.

Revanth Reddy's approach offers valuable lessons in political leadership. His empathy and respect for others foster enduring relationships, while his focus on collaboration strengthens alliances and paves the way for effective governance. His resilience in navigating challenges underscores the importance of patience and determination in political life.

Revanth Reddy's ability to manage political relationships showcases his leadership qualities and provides insights into effective governance and coalition-building. His journey highlights the significance of diplomacy, adaptability, and a vision-driven approach in politics, serving as an inspiring example for leaders aiming to create meaningful and transformative change.

CHAPTER NINETEEN

Engaging with stakeholders

Revanth Reddy, known for his charismatic leadership and strategic vision, has consistently demonstrated remarkable skill in engaging with stakeholders throughout his political career. As the Chief Minister of Telangana and a prominent leader in the Congress party, his approach to stakeholder engagement is rooted in collaboration, inclusivity, and clear communication. These qualities have enabled him to navigate complex political dynamics while fostering trust and unity among diverse groups.

A defining aspect of Revanth Reddy's leadership is his ability to forge strong alliances with political partners. His collaboration with the Communist Party of India (CPI) during the Telangana elections stands out as a prime example of his capacity to bring together diverse political ideologies under a shared vision. By focusing on common objectives, addressing mutual concerns, and ensuring transparent dialogue, he successfully built a coalition that challenged the ruling establishment and achieved electoral success. This ability to align ideologies and build trust highlights his strategic approach to stakeholder engagement.

Revanth's connection with the grassroots level is another cornerstone of his leadership. He maintains an active presence among the people through frequent public meetings, where he listens to grievances and addresses pressing issues such as farmers' welfare, unemployment, and public health. His proactive approach to understanding and resolving public concerns has strengthened his rapport with citizens, fostering trust and confidence in his governance. This grassroots connection reflects his commitment to inclusive leadership that prioritizes the needs of the people.

Within the Congress party, he places significant emphasis on empowering grassroots workers and local leaders. By involving them in decision-making processes and valuing their contributions, he ensures that they feel respected and motivated. This empowerment not only strengthens the party's foundation but also creates a network of dedicated leaders who represent the party's vision across constituencies. His inclusive leadership style encourages participation and collaboration, making every member feel like a vital part of the organization.

His openness to collaboration extends beyond politics. He actively engages with civil society organizations, advocacy groups, and intellectuals to address pressing social issues. By seeking input from diverse voices, he ensures that policies reflect the broader needs of Telangana's population. This willingness to collaborate with various stakeholders underscores his inclusive approach to governance, where collective wisdom is harnessed to drive meaningful change.

Inclusive policy-making is central to his vision for Telangana. While drafting policies, he ensures the involvement of stakeholders from various sectors, including farmers, industrialists, youth, and women. By considering the perspectives of different communities, he creates policies that are holistic and responsive to the state's diverse needs. This inclusivity has resulted in governance that resonates with the aspirations of the people, further solidifying his leadership.

He also recognizes the power of technology in engaging with stakeholders. His active presence on social media and digital platforms allows him to connect with a broader audience, particularly the youth. By sharing updates, soliciting feedback, and addressing concerns online, he has made himself accessible and relatable to the tech-savvy generation. This innovative approach to engagement ensures that his leadership remains relevant in an increasingly digital world.

The results of Revanth Reddy's stakeholder engagement are evident in his achievements. His alliance with the CPI was instrumental in uniting opposition forces against the ruling party, leading to Congress's victory in the elections. His consistent efforts to address public grievances have earned him the trust and support of Telangana's citizens. Additionally, his inclusive engagement strategies have resulted in policies that reflect the state's diverse needs, strengthening his reputation as a forward-thinking leader.

Revanth Reddy's approach to stakeholder engagement offers valuable lessons in leadership. Active listening fosters trust and collaboration by ensuring that stakeholders feel heard and understood. Transparency in communication builds alignment and reduces the potential for misunderstandings. Collaboration over competition amplifies impact and achieves larger goals by bringing together diverse groups. Lastly, adaptability in tailoring strategies to meet the unique needs of stakeholders ensures effectiveness and relevance.

Through his ability to balance diverse interests and build meaningful relationships, Revanth Reddy exemplifies how effective stakeholder engagement can drive collective progress. His leadership serves as an inspiring blueprint for inclusive and participatory governance, demonstrating the power of collaboration and empathy in achieving transformative change.

CHAPTER TWENTY

Crafting a public image

Revanth Reddy, the Chief Minister of Telangana, has meticulously crafted a public image that resonates with people from all walks of life. His persona is rooted in accessibility, dynamism, and progressive thinking, making him a standout figure in the political landscape. Central to his approach is his unwavering connection to the grassroots, where he frequently engages with farmers, youth, and marginalized communities. These interactions allow him to understand their concerns deeply, ensuring his leadership reflects empathy and a commitment to addressing their needs. This grassroots connection has solidified his reputation as a leader who truly resonates with the common people.

A trademark of Revanth Reddy's public image is his progressive vision for Telangana. His focus on development, innovation, and welfare schemes has positioned him as a reformist leader dedicated to the holistic growth of the state. Whether through initiatives in agriculture, education, or infrastructure, his forward-thinking policies cater to all sections of society, reinforcing his credibility as a leader with a mission to transform Telangana into a hub of opportunity and progress.

Communication plays a pivotal role in shaping his public image. Known for his sharp oratory skills, he delivers speeches that are both assertive and relatable, striking a chord with audiences in both rural and urban areas. His ability to articulate his vision and connect emotionally with the public enhances his appeal and ensures his message reaches every corner of the state. Coupled with his dynamic leadership style, which emphasizes decisive action and hands-on governance, he projects an image of a proactive and courageous leader. Whether it is addressing critical issues or responding to crises, his approach showcases his readiness to lead from the front and tackle challenges head-on.

Revanth Reddy's commitment to youth engagement further strengthens his image as a leader for the future. By prioritizing employment opportunities, skill development, and entrepreneurial initiatives, he positions himself as a champion of the younger generation. His ability to tap into the aspirations of youth and provide platforms for their growth ensures he remains relevant in an evolving political and social environment.

In the digital age, Revanth Reddy leverages social media effectively to communicate his ideas, achievements, and policies. His active online presence ensures he stays connected with a tech-savvy audience, making him approachable and accessible. Through digital platforms, he amplifies his vision and accomplishments, ensuring his leadership resonate across diverse demographics.

Underlying his public image is a strong foundation of political integrity. Revanth's commitment to accountability and transparency in governance sets him apart as a trustworthy leader. Despite facing challenges in his political journey, his resilience and determination shine through, reinforcing his credibility and earning the trust of the people.

Revanth Reddy's multifaceted approach is to shape his public image underscores his strategic vision, empathetic leadership, and ability to connect with diverse stakeholders. His grassroots connection, progressive policies, effective communication, and focus on youth and transparency collectively define his persona as a leader who is not only attuned to the needs of his people but also committed to driving transformative change in Telangana.

CHAPTER TWENTY-ONE

Handling Criticism and Challenges

Revanth Reddy's rise to political prominence has been accompanied by significant criticism and challenges, which he has tackled with resilience, strategy, and adaptability. Throughout his journey, he has faced allegations of corruption and various controversies, yet he has consistently addressed these accusations with conviction and transparency. Rather than retreating, he has emphasized his unwavering commitment to public service, often questioning the motives behind such allegations. By maintaining his composure and countering these claims with clarity, he has successfully deflected criticism while reinforcing his credibility.

Revanth Reddy's assertive political style has been instrumental in navigating criticism. He does not hesitate to challenge his detractors, using facts, sharp rhetoric, and public platforms to counter opposition narratives. In doing so, he often transforms criticism into an opportunity to highlight his achievements and underline his vision for progress. This ability to turn adversity into an advantage has become a hallmark of his political strategy, earning him respect as a determined and focused leader.

A key aspect of his approach to managing criticism is his direct engagement with the public. By connecting with people through rallies, media interactions, and social platforms, he ensures that his stance is clearly communicated to the masses. This grassroots approach not only allows him to clarify misconceptions but also helps him build trust among his supporters. His proactive engagement demonstrates his accessibility and strengthens his bond with the people of Telangana.

His adaptability to changing political dynamics has been another cornerstone of his leadership. Navigating complex landscapes, including internal party dynamics and opposition challenges, he has shown an impressive ability to build coalitions and find common ground. This strategic mindset allows him to overcome obstacles and maintain a strong foothold in Telangana's political arena.

The use of traditional and digital media has further empowered Revanth to manage criticism effectively. By leveraging these platforms, he shifts the focus from negative narratives to his policies and initiatives, ensuring that his achievements remain at the forefront. His strong media presence reinforces his image as a visionary leader and keeps him connected with diverse audiences.

Revanth Reddy's openness to criticism sets him apart as a pragmatic leader. Instead of dismissing criticism outright, he embraces it as feedback, using it to refine his strategies and enhance his governance. This willingness to learn and adapt not only strengthens his leadership but also portrays him as a grounded and self-aware individual.

Challenges and adversities have often fuelled his determination. His perseverance during politically tough times and legal hurdles highlights his resilience and commitment to his goals. By turning obstacles into milestones, he has proven his ability to rise above difficulties and emerge stronger. This tenacity has earned him admiration even from his critics and solidified his standing as a leader with an unwavering focus on his objectives.

Amidst criticism, he prioritizes uniting his supporters by reinforcing his vision for a progressive Telangana. By focusing on shared goals and addressing public concerns, he strengthens his base and ensures their continued trust and loyalty. This ability to rally support during challenging times further underscores his effectiveness as a leader.

Revanth Reddy's journey exemplifies the qualities of a resilient and strategic politician who thrives in the face of adversity. Through transparency, adaptability, and a deep connection with the people, he has not only overcome criticism but also used it as a stepping stone to greater achievements. His ability to navigate challenges with poise and determination continues to shape his legacy as a transformative leader.

CHAPTER TWENTY-TWO

Leveraging Social Media

Revanth Reddy has harnessed the power of social media as a key tool in shaping his political career and engaging with citizens. By strategically utilizing platforms such as Twitter, Facebook, Instagram, and YouTube, he has managed to connect with a wide and diverse audience, enhancing his public image and solidifying his role as a leader who is accessible and in tune with the people.

One of the key advantages of social media for Revanth Reddy is the ability to communicate directly with the public, bypassing the traditional media filters. Through these platforms, he shares real-time updates on policies, initiatives, and his political journey, offering a transparent view into his leadership. This direct engagement fosters trust and establishes him as an approachable figure, unmediated by the biases of mainstream media.

Revanth Reddy's use of social media also allows him to respond to pressing issues in real time. Whether it's addressing a public grievance or commenting on critical national and state events, his timely posts reflect his proactive leadership style. This immediate response not only demonstrates his awareness of current issues but also positions him as a leader who is on the ground, tackling concerns head-on.

In addition to responding to issues, he leverages social media to showcase his government's achievements and development initiatives. Through visually appealing posts, info graphics, and videos, he highlights progress in areas like infrastructure, education, and healthcare. These posts not only keep citizens informed but also strengthen his image as a progressive leader committed to the development of Telangana.

Understanding the influence of social media on younger demographics, he tailors his content to resonate with millennial. His focus on issues such as education, employment, and innovation aligns with the aspirations of the youth, further enhancing his appeal to this vital constituency. This targeted approach helps him to establish himself as a leader who is forward-thinking and attuned to the concerns of the younger generation.

During election cycles and public campaigns, he effectively amplifies his message through hash tags, live streams, and interactive posts, creating momentum and generating widespread participation. His ability to mobilize supporters and rally participation using social media is a testament to his understanding of modern political communication and the power of digital engagement.

Social media also serves as a platform for him to counter opposition narratives and address criticism. By presenting facts and engaging with detractors constructively, he is able to neutralize negative coverage and clarify his stance on contentious issues. This direct and transparent engagement helps him to control the narrative and present his side of the story, bolstering his credibility.

Beyond political issues, Revanth Reddy uses social media to advocate for various causes such as farmer welfare, women empowerment, and environmental sustainability. By positioning himself as a socially responsible leader, he broadens his appeal to different sections of society, reinforcing his commitment to the well-being of the people of Telangana.

He also uses social media for visual storytelling, sharing photos, videos, and personal stories that humanize him and make him more relatable. These glimpses into his personal life, combined with his political journey, help create an approachable and down-to-earth image, strengthening his connection with the public.

Collaborating with influencers, journalists, and thought leaders on social media further amplifies his message, extending his reach and enhancing his credibility. By engaging with key figures in various fields, he broadens his influence and ensures that his voice reaches a larger audience, contributing to the growth of his public image.

Through the effective use of social media, Revanth Reddy has transformed it into a powerful tool for communication, engagement, and political mobilization. His ability to connect with citizens directly, showcase his achievements, and advocate for important causes has strengthened his position as a dynamic and relatable leader.

CHAPTER TWENTY-THREE

Significant Achievements

Revanth Reddy's political career is defined by a series of remarkable achievements that have solidified his reputation as a transformative leader in Telangana. His journey to political prominence is a proof to his unwavering dedication, strategic vision, and deep-rooted connection with the people. One of his most significant milestones is his rise to the position of Chief Minister of Telangana, a role he secured through his effective leadership and determination. Despite facing considerable political obstacles, his ability to connect with grassroots communities and his vision for the state's development were key factors in his ascension to this position.

A major focus of his leadership has been the welfare of farmers, a cause that has earned him widespread recognition. His efforts to improve the lives of farmers in Telangana have been both comprehensive and impactful. His initiatives, including the introduction of subsidized irrigation systems, crop insurance schemes, and the revival of traditional water conservation practices, have greatly benefited the agricultural community. These actions reflect his understanding of the issues facing rural Telangana and his commitment to addressing them.

In addition to his focus on agriculture, he has been a strong advocate for the youth of Telangana, particularly in terms of employment and skill development. His flagship program, "Skill Up Telangana," has provided numerous job opportunities for young people, enhancing their employability and skill sets. his engagement with the youth has made him a popular figure among younger voters, who see him as a leader who understands their needs and aspirations.

Infrastructure development has been another area where he has left a lasting impact. Under his leadership, Telangana has witnessed rapid infrastructural growth, with significant improvements in roads, bridges, and irrigation projects. His emphasis on urban planning and rural development has strengthened the state's connectivity and improved the quality of life for its citizens. These infrastructural advancements are seen as crucial to the state's future prosperity and have bolstered his image as a visionary leader.

Women's empowerment has also been a key priority for Revanth Reddy. Through a variety of policies that promote education, healthcare, and entrepreneurship among women, he has empowered countless women across the state. Programs like interest-free loans for women-led businesses have provided women with the resources to start and grow their own enterprises, contributing to economic development and gender equality in Telangana.

His commitment to education is another defining feature of his leadership. He has introduced reforms aimed at improving the quality of education in the state, including the establishment of new schools and colleges and the provision of scholarships for underprivileged students.

These initiatives reflect his belief that education is the key to unlocking the potential of the next generation and ensuring a brighter future for Telangana.

Environmental conservation has been an area where he has made significant strides. He has launched several initiatives focused on sustainability, including Afforestation drives, water conservation programs, and solar energy projects. These efforts not only help protect Telangana's natural resources but also align with his broader vision of sustainable development for the state. His focus on the environment has earned him respect as a leader who is mindful of the long-term implications of growth and development.

He has also focused on improving public welfare and healthcare. His government introduced comprehensive healthcare schemes to ensure that medical services are affordable and accessible to all citizens. Initiatives such as mobile clinics and the improvement of hospital infrastructure have strengthened the state's healthcare system and ensured that the most vulnerable populations receive adequate care.

Another significant achievement of Revanth Reddy has been his work in resolving land disputes and protecting public assets. He has played an instrumental role in reclaiming encroached lands and ensuring that they are used for the public good. His efforts to resolve these disputes have contributed to the overall development and well-being of the state, further solidifying his reputation as a leader who prioritizes public welfare.

Lastly, his commitment to fostering unity and diversity in Telangana has been a hallmark of his leadership. He has worked tirelessly to ensure that the state respects its cultural and linguistic diversity, creating an inclusive environment where all citizens feel valued and respected. This focus on unity has helped build a sense of pride among the people of Telangana, strengthening the social fabric of the state.

Through his leadership, Revanth Reddy has made significant strides in transforming Telangana into a more developed, inclusive, and prosperous state. His achievements in various sectors, from farmers' welfare to infrastructure development and women's empowerment, have earned him respect as a visionary and resilient leader. Revanth's political journey serves as an inspiring example of perseverance, strategic thinking, and dedication to public service.

CHAPTER TWENTY-FOUR

Land Mark Policies

The Government of Telangana has introduced several welfare initiatives aimed at enhancing the socio-economic status of various sections of society, with particular focus on women, youth, and the protection of public assets. Among the key programs are the Mahalakshmi, Cheyutha, and Gruhalaxmi schemes, as well as the Yuva Vikasam initiative and the Hyderabad Disaster Response and Asset Monitoring and Protection Agency (HYDRA).

The Mahalakshmi Scheme, for instance, is designed to provide financial assistance to women in Telangana, with the primary goal of fostering their economic empowerment. Through direct financial transfers, eligible women are supported in their economic activities, including self-employment and business ventures. This initiative reflects the state's commitment to improving the socio-economic conditions of women by ensuring they are financially independent and actively contributing to the state's development.

Similarly, the Cheyutha Scheme is another crucial welfare program that focuses on women from disadvantaged communities such as backward classes, Scheduled Castes, Scheduled Tribes, and minorities. By offering financial aid, the government helps these women establish or improve their businesses, empowering them to become self-reliant and to play an active role in the economic growth of Telangana. This initiative addresses the systemic barriers that women from marginalized communities often face and provides them with opportunities for economic participation.

The Gruhalaxmi Scheme, on the other hand, is targeted at supporting women in rural areas by providing financial assistance for household expenses and improving living standards. The primary aim of this initiative is to reduce the financial burden on women, thereby enabling them to focus on the well-being of their families and communities. By offering financial resources to manage household needs, the Gruhalaxmi Scheme plays a vital role in enhancing the quality of life for rural women, promoting their financial independence and welfare.

The Yuva Vikasam initiative is focused on empowering the youth of Telangana by providing them with the necessary skills for employment and entrepreneurship. By offering skill development programs, training workshops, and educational initiatives, this program aims to equip the younger generation with the tools they need to secure jobs and contribute to the state's economic growth. The scheme also seeks to encourage entrepreneurship, enabling young people to create new opportunities for themselves and their communities.

Lastly, the Hyderabad Disaster Response and Asset Monitoring and Protection Agency (HYDRA) were established in 2024 to manage disaster response and protect public assets in the Hyderabad urban region. The agency's main responsibilities include monitoring and safeguarding public infrastructure such as parks, lakes, roads, and government buildings from encroachments.

HYDRA also plays a crucial role in managing disaster preparedness and response, ensuring that the city remains safe and resilient in the face of emergencies.

These initiatives reflect the Telangana government's comprehensive approach to welfare and development. By focusing on empowering women, providing opportunities for youth, and ensuring the protection of public assets, the state is laying the groundwork for long-term socio-economic progress.

CHAPTER TWENTY-FIVE

Turning Points in the career

Revanth Reddy's political career has been marked by several defining moments that propelled him from a local leader to the Chief Minister of Telangana. His journey began at the grassroots level, where his ability to connect with the rural population and address the pressing issues faced by farmers and marginalized communities laid the foundation for his political rise. This deep connection with the people, particularly those in rural areas, became a cornerstone of his leadership style, earning him the trust and support of his constituents.

One of the key turning points in Revanth's career came in 2009 when he won the MLA seat in the Kodangal constituency. Despite facing stiff competition, Revanth focused on solving local problems such as water scarcity and rural unemployment. His efforts to address these concerns won him widespread support, establishing him as a regional leader with a strong base among the people.

In 2017, Revanth made a significant move by switching from the Telugu Desam Party (TDP) to the Indian National Congress (INC). This decision was not without controversy, but it proved to be a strategic one. His alignment with the INC allowed him to work within a national framework and pursue his vision for Telangana more effectively. While the move faced criticism initially, it later proved to be a defining moment in his political ascent, providing him with the platform to further his political career.

Revanth's leadership abilities were further recognized in 2021 when he was appointed as the President of the Telangana Pradesh Congress Committee (TPCC). Under his leadership, the Congress Party in Telangana began to regain momentum, particularly among youth and rural voters. His efforts to revitalize the party and connect with the grassroots were instrumental in its resurgence, signalling a new phase in his leadership.

In 2022, he gained national attention for his aggressive stance on farmer issues. He became a vocal critic of policies that negatively impacted farmers, participating in protests and leading a historic sit-in at the state assembly. His unwavering commitment to championing the cause of farmers solidified his image as a leader of the people, further strengthening his political influence.

Finally, Revanth Reddy's leadership reached its pinnacle in 2024 when he led the Congress Party to a decisive victory in the Telangana Assembly elections. His strategic campaign, which focused on youth, women, and farmers, resonated with the people of Telangana, leading to his election as the Chief Minister of the state. This victory marked the culmination of years of hard work, perseverance, and dedication to the people of Telangana, establishing him as a transformative leader in the state's political history.

CHAPTER TWENTY-SIX

Final Reflections

The journey of Anumula Revanth Reddy is a witness to the power of perseverance, vision, and unyielding dedication. From his humble beginnings to his rise as a prominent political leader in Telangana, his story is one of resilience in the face of adversity, strategic thinking, and an unwavering commitment to the people he serves. His ability to connect with the grassroots, his innovative approach to governance, and his advocacy for social justice set him apart as a leader who truly understands the pulse of the masses.

Revanth Reddy's career reminds us that true leadership is not just about holding a position of power, but about making a real impact in the lives of people. It is about standing firm in the face of challenges, adapting to changing times, and always staying grounded in values of empathy and justice. His leadership is characterized by a balanced approach: the ability to drive change while remaining deeply connected to the community's needs.

As aspiring leaders, we can learn much from his journey. His story teaches us the importance of having a clear vision, of embracing challenges with resilience, and of leading with compassion. It is a reminder that leadership is not about personal glory, but about working tirelessly for the greater good of society.

In the end, Revanth Reddy's rise reflects the essence of perseverance—pushing forward despite obstacles, staying true to one's values, and striving for a better future for all. His life and career offer invaluable lessons on leadership, reminding us that greatness is not just achieved by talent or ambition alone, but by an unwavering commitment to one's principles and the well-being of others.